Old Greenwich Village

AN ARCHITECTURAL PORTRAIT

PHOTOGRAPHY BY

Steve Gross and Susan Daley

INTRODUCTION BY

Sam Tanenhaus

◆

A NORFLEET PRESS BOOK

THE PRESERVATION PRESS

NATIONAL TRUST FOR HISTORIC PRESERVATION

The Preservation Press
National Trust for Historic Preservation
1785 Massachusetts Avenue, N.W.
Washington, D.C. 20036

*The National Trust for Historic Preservation is the only private,
nonprofit organization chartered by Congress to encourage public
participation in the preservation of sites, buildings, and objects
significant in American history and culture. The National Trust carries out
this mission by fostering an appreciation of the diverse character and meaning
of our American cultural heritage and by preserving and revitalizing the livability
of our communities by leading the nation in saving America's historic environments.*

*Support for the National Trust is provided by membership dues, contributions,
and a matching grant from the National Park Service, U.S. Department of the Interior,
under provisions of the National Historic Preservation Act of 1966. The opinions expressed
here do not necessarily reflect the views or policies of the Interior Department.*

Composition by Browne Book Composition, Inc.
Printed on acid-free paper by Paramount Printers, Hong Kong

5 4 3 2 1 97 96 95 94 93

Library of Congress Cataloging-in-Publication Data

Gross, Steve.
Old Greenwich Village : an architectural portrait / photography by
Steve Gross and Susan Daley ; introduction by Sam Tanenhaus.
p.   cm.
"A Norfleet Press book"—T.p. verso
ISBN 0-89133-232-4 (cloth)   ISBN 0-89133-233-2 (paper)
1. Greenwich Village (New York, N.Y.)—Buildings, structures, etc. 2. New York (N.Y.)—
Buildings, structures, etc. 3. Architecture—New York (N.Y.) 1. Daley, Susan, 1953– . II. Title.
NA735.G75G76 1993
720'.9747'1—dc20   93-3234

A Norfleet Press Book
New York, New York

Director: John G. Tucker
Designer: Laury A. Egan
Editor: Carolyn L. Maxwell

*Frontispiece: Courtyard of Gertrude Vanderbuilt Whitney's studio,
Number 17½ MacDougal Alley*

This book is dedicated to the memory of
Tom Glauser, Mario Lavalle and Gerry LaBorde

Truly a Village

BY

Sam Tanenhaus

The shaping power of Greenwich Village begins with its crazy map, the twisted grid that stubbornly defies the Euclidean plan of uptown Manhattan and its tidy mortising of avenue and cross street. Village pathways obey no logical pattern. They bend and veer in unexpected directions. Only in the Village will you find yourself at the intersection of 4th and 12th Streets—blocks supposed to be parallel—or at the juncture of two streets each named Waverly Place.

It is this eccentricity that has enabled the Village to remain, after two centuries, truly a village, with narrow alleys and weedy lanes, tranquil churchyards and gated mews. Even its busiest intersection, Sheridan Square, where traffic converges from six different angles, offers the sanctuary of Christopher Park, a tiny wedge of garden, profuse with color (save in winter) and overtopped by leafy sycamores.

Situated north of Houston Street and south of Union Square, the Village occupies the widest bulge of Manhattan Island and so has a feel more horizontal than vertical. Uncluttered by high rises, it enjoys a comforting dominion of sky, an opulence of sun and shadow, a direct imprint of the seasons.

This outdoorsiness recovers something of the Village's origins, for it was marshland when first settled in the 1600s by Dutch and English colonists, who methodically groomed the sodden ground. By the mid-18th century, Greenwich was home to large estates. Many of these survived the Revolutionary War but soon after were subdivided and parceled out to yeoman farmers, Jeffersonian rustics who wanted little contact with the urban tumult of the Battery, two miles to the south.

As the city branched northward from its southern tip, Greenwich remained a place apart, complete unto itself. Just how complete became evident in 1811, when city fathers, drunk with futurity, drew up a grid for the whole of Manhattan. Their blueprints included a remapped Greenwich, its winding lanes unbent. Greenwich locals protested and were granted an exemption: the area west of Sixth Avenue was left to pursue its ungeometric course. The terrain to the east, later subsumed by the Village, was mapped along more rigid lines.

Meanwhile, New York kept growing. By the 1810s, it was a true city—a port city, with filthy docks and infested streets. In the summer of 1822, yellow fever sent a panicked throng, some sixty thousand, swarming up Manhattan to the airy shelter of Greenwich. Once the crisis subsided, most of the invaders retreated—but others preferred their new surroundings and stayed behind. Within two decades, the local population had quadrupled and Greenwich's small farms were supplanted by close ranks of rowhouses.

One portion of land, however, remained untouched, the swampy plot that was to become Washington Square, the Village's most public park, its central *piazza*. It evolved slowly. In 1780, the city purchased eight acres from a private estate and converted them to a public gallows and potter's field. (The "hanging tree," a stalwart elm, was retired from service in 1819, but still stands in a northwest corner of the square.) In 1826, after some twenty thousand corpses had been interred, the field was made the parade ground of the National Guard. It was not an ideal site; horse-drawn artillery sometimes sank into the shallow graves. By 1850, the plot had been transformed yet again—into a prototype of the park we know today, with its fountain and walkways and handsome plantings: buttonwoods, gingkoes, and catalpas.

In 1892, Washington Square received its crowning adornment—the memorial arch designed by Stanford White. Ten days after construction began, workmen's shovels scraped against the skulls, and then the skeletons, of bodies buried more than a hundred years before. In Greenwich Village, the sovereignty of the past is as real as blackened bones.

◆

The Village's architectural history is equally, if less pungently, haunted by time. Sometimes the past survives only in a fanlight, lintel, or cornice. But many structures have endured in their entirety—fine examples of Federalist, Greek Revival, Neo-Gothic, and Italianate buildings that together compose a résumé of American architecture in the middle decades of the nineteenth century. Newer styles have been added over the years—French Empire and Romanesque in the late nineteenth century, Beaux Arts and Art Deco in the early twentieth.

The oldest and most picturesque precinct begins west of Sixth Avenue. This is the West Village, its earnest-sounding streets (Morton, Jones, Barrow) graced with brick-faced Federalist houses which, after seventeen decades, have relaxed into an agreeable off-plumbness. Their doors, topped by semi-circular fanlights and framed by delicate colonnettes, stand as signatures for the buildings and the period.

Grove Street has a row of tiny two-story homes, each crowned with a single large dormer. Number 17 Grove, at the corner of Bedford, is altogether different in design. A wood-frame house built in 1822, it anticipates the elegance of a different time and place: it could be the bank president's mansion in Dodge City. Next door is 102 Bedford, known as "Twin Peaks." It went up in the 1830s but acquired its gingerbread exterior nearly a century later, in the Roaring Twenties.

Near its terminus at Hudson Street, Grove becomes a bower of monastic quiet. Gaunt-trunked ailanthus trees tilt up from the buckled pavement; thick beards of ivy tug at the prim lintels. There is a point where the street suddenly crooks, leaving you at a small locked gate. It guards a courtyard carpeted with pachysandra. Set back from it are six attached dwellings, all painted burgundy, each with white shutters. It is an undisturbed picture of a vanished era, summoned from the mid 19th century, when the row was inhabited by laborers at the local breweries and called Mixed Ale Alley. Today, this cul-de-sac is one of the Village's choicest addresses, its name upgraded to Grove Court.

There are also treasures to be found east of Sixth Avenue. A group of splendid Greek Revival town-houses stands on Washington Square North. Collectively known as the "Row," they belong today to New York University, which has converted them to administrative offices. But the toned-brick exteriors, with their tall shuttered windows and bright flower boxes, still have a patrician flavor. As a child, Henry James often visited his grandmother at Number 19. Later, he would evoke its varnished parlors in his novel *Washington Square* (1881). Its heroine, dim, doomed Catherine Sloper, had been raised on the Row in a home built to her father's exacting standards. James's description of it is famous:

> The ideal of quiet and of genteel retirement, in 1835, was found in Washington Square, where the Doctor built himself a handsome, modern, wide-fronted house, with a big balcony before the drawing room windows, and a flight of white marble steps ascending to a portal which was also faced with white marble. This structure, and many of its neighbors, which it exactly resembled, were supposed . . . to embody the last results of architectural science, and they remain to this day very solid and honorable dwellings . . . I know not whether it is owing to the tenderness of early associations, but this portion of New York appears to many persons the most delectable. It has a kind of established repose which is not of frequent occurrence in other quarters of the long, shrill city; it has a riper, richer, more honorable look than any of the upper ramifications of the great longitudinal thoroughfare [Fifth Avenue]—the look of having had something of a social history.

The Village's social history extends back, in truth, to the beginnings of the Republic. Tom Paine died in 1809 on the site now occupied by Marie's Crisis Café, the piano bar at 59 Grove Street. His buoyant declaration, "We have it in our power to begin the world over again" could stand as the motto for many generations of Village rebels.

Paine's spiritual heirs included Walt Whitman, who in the 1850s crossed over to Manhattan on the Brooklyn ferry to spend evenings at Pfaff's, a basement beer hall on lower Broadway. He mixed with a clientele mostly in their twenties, a "ragtag crowd of artists, actors, and literary people" as well as "free lovers, radicals, and vegetarians," according to Paul Zweig, one of Whitman's biographers.

Whitman was senior to most other habitués at Pfaff's (he turned 40 in 1859) and was something of a celebrity; he had published a notorious book of verse, *Leaves of Grass,* that proclaimed a new American idiom: ecstatic, egotistical, and frankly sexual. Some readers were alarmed: "Who is this arrogant young man," one reviewer wondered, "who proclaims himself Poet of Time, and who roots like a pig among the rotten garbage of licentious thoughts?" Whitman did indeed dwell on

> Love-thoughts, love-juice, love-odor, love-yielding,
> love-climbers, and the climbing sap,
> Arms and hands of love, lips of love, phallic thumb of love,
> breast of love, bellies press'd and glued together with love.

In "the vault of Pfaff's," the poet harnessed his effusions. His job was to watch and to listen. He was fascinated by the physicians, released from their late-night shifts at nearby New York Hospital, who arrived bearing tales rich in gruesome particulars.

In expansive moments, while surveying the crowd, Whitman realized, perhaps, that the tavern was less vault than incubator. New specimens were being hatched, warmed under the candles, nourished by heaping platters and foaming tankards—the authentic progeny of the New York he found so stirring, the city of "tall-topt marble and iron beauties," of "swarming market places," of rich immigrant tonalities woven into a "nest of languages."

◊

By the time of Whitman's death in 1892, New York *was* urban America. No other city boasted such size and ethnic variety, such excesses of wealth and poverty and crime, so wide a palette of dangers and allures. It was half pageant, half *Grand Guignol,* an empire of commerce, built in stone, and massed with citizens who dashed up and down the avenues in horse-drawn vehicles, purposeful as conquerors.

Just how far New York had come—or descended—was evident to Henry James in 1904, when he returned after a twenty-year absence. The smallish port city of his birth, its commerce and population all clustered near downtown docks, was now a "vast, crude democracy of trade." Manhattan's architecture, "impudently new," was ruled by "multitudinous skyscrapers standing up . . . like extravagant pins in a cushion already overplanted, and stuck in as in the dark, anywhere and anyhow."

From another angle, the skyline resembled a "broken hair-comb turned up." James preferred the comb's gaps to its teeth and sought refuge in the Village's congenial proportions. Traipsing through the remembered streets, he gratefully registered "no new note in the picture, not one, for instance, when I paused before a low house in a small row on the south side of Waverly Place . . . with its mere two storeys, its lowly 'stoop,' its dislocated ironwork of the forties, the early fifties, the record, in its face, of blistering summers and of the long stages of the loss of self-respect." The bordering neighborhoods might be unrecognizable, but the Village remained "as consummate a morsel of the old liquor-scented, heated-looking city, the city of no pavements . . . as I could have desired."

"Loss of self-respect" was a polite way of saying the Village had gone to seed. Its "housing stock," according to a later account, "had grown dilapidated and slum tenements, brothels, and drab manufactories encroached side streets . . . south and north of Washington Square." The elite families fled to safer havens, the impregnable mansions and luxury apartment buildings of upper Fifth Avenue. Their departure left a vacuum soon filled by immigrants (Irish, German, and Italian), "many of whom took shelter in the boardinghouses and hastily partitioned cold-water flats that materialized in recently vacated houses. An intriguing shabbiness soon descended on Greenwich Village."

Intriguing to whom? To yet another wave of immigrants, refugees from America itself, from its heartland—the cow towns and mining camps, the bone-hard church pews and cheerless temperance halls. Some restless souls pined for Europe and its citadels of culture. Others longed for New York:

> I'd heard about the Village. There was a Greenwich Village girl in Seattle—a little Roumanian Jewess. I got to know her when I left the woods and lived with her while I was sick. She had painted fans and things—I'd never seen anything like that. So finally I came to the Village. I did sewing. Now I run this little store, and I like it, because I always had a sort of an original taste in decorations and things. I make these blouses myself—they're not afraid of having them too bright down here. Another thing is that nobody cares what you do down here—nobody expects you to cook or to go to church—and you can always talk to interesting people. I tell you, the West is all right, but it's a great relief to get some place where you can feel a little bit free. I know all about those great open spaces.

These sentences conclude a monologue, "The Road to Greenwich Village," written by Edmund Wilson in 1925. The "sketch," as he called it, was taken "from life." If you visited Greenwich Village, Wilson implied, you would meet many persons like this one, transplanted Westerners who spoke in frontier cadences. This woman's tone is, in fact, reminiscent of Huck Finn's. Like Huck, she had felt hemmed in at home, ganged up against, menaced by piety; like him, she was faintly oddballish, didn't fit in. But unlike Huck, she was conscious of having "a sort of original taste."

Other American provincials had even larger appetites. They came to New York convinced their "original taste" was the insignia of larval genius, the marking of a special destiny. They found soulmates in the cafés and taverns, and excitedly held forth on big topics—art and politics. And then, talked out, they stumbled home to the Village's partitioned flats where they bunked like ranch hands.

By 1910, Greenwich Village had become the Latin Quarter for an entire nation, crowded with artists, visionaries, enthusiasts, debaters. They differed from the usual run of native types yet were, in their way, highly American—hard workers and unabashed self-promoters. The surest Village talents spent long, honest hours at the easel or writing desk and then bounded out the door to hustle their wares, barging into Alfred Stieglitz's midtown gallery with an armful of paintings or bushwhacking the editor of a "little magazine" with a stack of poems. There was a precedent for such opportunism. Hadn't Whitman published anonymous reviews extolling his own poetry?

The best of the magazines was *Masses*, with offices (as of 1913) on Greenwich Avenue. Its editors opened their pages to "entertainment, education, and the  livelier kinds of propaganda." The main thing was not to be boring. Noisy editorial meetings were held once a month at an artist's studio, most often Art Young's or John Sloan's, where by democratic wrangle the next month's issue was planned. The contents were consistently "exuberant, shocking, and stirring," wrote Theodore Draper in *The Roots of American Communism*. "Serious verse, essays, propaganda, drawings, satire, and slapstick were jumbled together. A list of [its] contributors reads like a *Who's Who* of artistic and literary America for the next two decades or more."

The Village, now dubbed the "Republic of Washington Square," even had a First Lady, the ceremonious Mabel Dodge. She came to New York in the winter of 1912 after several years in Florence. There she had bought and beautified a *quattrocento* mansion, the Villa Curonia. She ornamented its copious rooms with choice guests—the aristocratic, the gifted—and decorated her garden with a pair of white peacocks. Eventually, this diversion palled. The guests grew bored, and perhaps the peacocks, too. The hostess, fully Europeanized, sailed to the United States (she had been born in Buffalo) with dread, steeled for "ugliness." She rationed herself four spacious rooms at 23 Fifth Avenue, north of Washington Square, and redid them in a minimalist motif. Everything was white: woodwork, wallpaper, curtains; the fireplace was faced with white marble.

Enthroned in an armchair, Dodge awaited the arrival of Interesting People.

They visited out of curiosity, lingered out of gratitude, and gladly came back. The hostess was, as Lincoln Steffens wrote, "one of the most wonderful things in the world . . . an aristocratic, rich, good-looking woman," ethereal in her flowing gowns. Dodge's "Evenings" have been characterized as "a combination of town meeting, Chautauqua, and cocktail party."

They also constituted the Village's first salon, never surpassed, for Dodge gathered her guests at a peak cultural moment, when the tide of Modernism, rising in Europe, was poised to break on American shores. There were sweeping new movements in painting (Cubism), poetry (Imagism), and politics (Bolshevism). One evening in 1914, Walter Lippmann, a prodigy four years out of Harvard, guided the throng through the theories of Sigmund Freud, said to be the first such parlor discussion held in the United States.

A regular at 23 Fifth Avenue was Lippmann's Harvard classmate John Reed, "a mad playboy with a streak of poetry," as John Dos Passos later described him. In 1911, "Jack" Reed rented a flat on Washington Square South and, more playboy than poet, poured forth callow rhymes:

> This spawning filth, these monuments uncouth
> Are but her wild, ungovernable youth.
> But the sky-scrapers, dwarfing earthly things,
> Ah, that is how she sings!

Reed was a Westerner from Portland, Oregon. It was a long way from there to Harvard, and a long way from the Village to Mexico, where in 1913 he went to observe its "romantic revolution," as Granville Hicks put it in his hagiography, *John Reed.* Mexico's rebel hero, Pancho Villa, took a liking to Reed and gave him exclusive interviews. Reed was entranced. "He could not resist identifying himself with underdogs," wrote Theodore Draper, "especially if they followed strong, ruthless leaders." The dispatches Reed sent home to *The World,* a New York daily, and to *The Metropolitan,* a socialist journal, were unashamedly partisan and decidedly more lyrical than his verse.

Mexico was just a warm-up. In 1917, Reed hastened to Petrograd to report on a much bigger revolution. Inevitably, he joined the Bolsheviks and basked in the triumph of their *coup d'état,* "the long-thwarted rise of the Russian masses," as Hicks wrote. Reed himself, thwarted fatally by typhus at age thirty-three, was buried in 1920 near the Kremlin Wall. He died the Village's preeminent modern hero, its swashbuckler.

◆

With the advent of World War I, the Village's "social history" shifted course. "Quiet" and "genteel retirement" no longer seemed possible, or desirable, in the cramped, crooked streets, teeming now with unleashed energies and "alien" enthusiasms—political, aesthetic, sexual. In 1917, when *Masses* denounced America's entry in the war, it was officially suppressed and four of its editors— Reed, Max Eastman, Floyd Dell, and Art Young—stood trial for unpatriotism. The phrase "Greenwich Village radical" entered the national idiom, along with "Greenwich Village artist" and "Greenwich Village type," all uttered as often in scorn as in praise. Villagers were pleased. They courted disapproval—what better proof that they had discovered a brave new world, had reached what Edmund Wilson was to call "the shores of light"?

By the 1920s, the Village had become, observed Malcolm Cowley, a poet and critic back from the war, "not only a place, a mood, a way of life," but "also a doctrine . . . a system of ideas." *System* seems antithetical to "the idea of salvation of the child," "the idea of paganism," and "the idea of liberty." But these vaporous tenets did solidify into a plausible whole, an exuberant "crusade against puritanism" that traced its origins to Whitman, and earlier to Paine. Some of the crusading was faddish (women smoking cigars), some woolly-headed (the "practical mysticism" of G.I. Gurdjieff), and some of it lethal (Bolshevism). But the revolt was real and staked the Village's boundaries as decisively as did Washington Square Arch.

The most serious experiments were aesthetic. The Village was especially hospitable to poets. In the 1920s, Hart Crane launched his grand lyric flights from 45 Grove Street, and e.e. cummings lived on Patchin Place in digs that were, Cowley remembered, "a model of squalor." Edna St. Vincent Millay, siren of exotic romanticism, flitted glamorously through the passageways of 75½ Bedford Street. A mere nine-and-a-half feet wide, it was the narrowest house in all the Village, but roomy enough to hold her famous candle—the one she lighted at both ends.

But what happened once the flame guttered out? Wasn't there something forced in all this gaiety? "Free love" had begun to pall and Prohibition booze was inducing *delirium tremens.* By decade's end, the raucous laughter had died. In 1929, Lionel Trilling, age twenty-four, rented rooms on Bank Street across the way from Edmund Wilson, one of his idols. It was a bold first step, but was it  belated? Even as Trilling inhaled the heady scent of bohemia, he feared the Village's "great days" lay in the past.

It was natural to think so in 1929, for by then the national hangover had begun. By 1932, the nadir of the Depression, Americans' total income was one-half of what it had been four years earlier. Yet the Village bore up well. Marginalized even in the best of times, bohemia is indurated to economic hardship.

And so it thrived, with adjustments. The ideological "system" had, of course, to be overhauled. Hedonism and paganism, now passé, were replaced by doctrinaire and militant Politics. It was the scale on which all ideas were weighed, all personal conduct measured. The joyous hodgepodge of *Masses* would no longer do. Its drab successor, *New Masses,* was a Communist organ: no democratic jumbling allowed.

It seemed as if all New York, and especially the Village, "dreamed of leaving North America and merging with Soviet Russia," wrote Saul Bellow, an apprentice writer from Chicago who migrated to the Village in the late 1930s. Some Villagers did more than dream. Whittaker Chambers, *New Masses* editor and ascendant star of the literary left, quit writing altogether to join a Soviet spy ring, helping develop microfilm in the bathtub of a Gay Street rowhouse. Later an apostate and later still an informer, he denounced his one-time comrades in the hearing rooms of the House Committee on Un-American Activities.

The Village had long been hospitable to conspirators: In 1917, mere months before the Bolshevik Revolution, Leon Trotsky worked in a "dingy hole" of an office at 77 St. Mark's Place. With perfect symmetry, this address was later home to W. H. Auden, whose poem, "September 1, 1939," placed the tombstone on the romance of revolutionism. Reviewing the thirties, Auden beheld "a low dishonest decade," all its "clever hopes expire[d]" in the ashes of the next world war.

◆

The ideologies died but high causes remained. In 1938, a jazz *aficionado*, Barney Josephson, opened Café Society at One Sheridan Square. It was New York's first integrated music club. Lena Horne sang there, and Billie Holiday. Benny Goodman led a trio featuring a black pianist, Teddy Wilson. The club closed its doors in 1950, but by then jazz had infiltrated other Village art experiments—the novels of Jack Kerouac, the poems of Allen Ginsberg, the action paintings of Jackson Pollock. While these innovators owed much, in theory, to the automatism of the Surrealists, their creative processes resembled the high-wire improvisations of saxophonist Charlie Parker. There was something new in all this, a defiance not only of aesthetic convention, but also of the Village's own past, its rigid fealty to High Art.

Unlike their predecessors, American artists who came of age after World War II saw their country not as a province of Europe, but as the seat of world culture. They grew up inspired by native forms—jazz and film—and went on to develop another, Abstract Expressionism. American art was now studiously mimicked in those foreign capitals once considered the source of all new ideas. The Village, so long the receiver and transmitter of artistic impulses, began to point its antennae in a new direction, west—toward, of all places, the heartland.

Refugees still arrived, not as roughhewn provincials, however, but as heralds and prophets. When Bob Dylan, not yet twenty, came to the Village from Minnesota, he flunked his first audition. People wanted folk music, he was told, not the "hillbilly" songs he sang. But those songs contained the germ of a new sound, one that flourished in Village clubs throughout the 1960s.

In 1964, Sam Shepard, another arrival from the hinterlands, was waiting tables at the Village Gate (the jazz club on Bleecker Street) when on impulse he wrote *Cowboys.* Many more scripts followed and they established Shepard as the legitimate heir to an earlier Village dramatist, Eugene O'Neill.

The Village did not make Shepard an artist; it released the artist in him. In other cases, in other times, the results were not as happy. Beneath the triumphs

lies a crowded potter's field. There is Edgar Allan Poe, who lived at 85 West Third Street in 1845 and died four years later near a Baltimore saloon at age 40. There is Delmore Schwartz, brilliant, learned, and handsome, the reputed "Mozart of talkers." At age twenty-two, while living in a furnished room off Washington Square, he wrote a magnificent short story, "In Dreams Begin Responsibilities," but even then was bedeviled by the paranoia that later undid him. And there is Dylan Thomas, who poisoned himself with a last martini at the White Horse Tavern on Hudson Street (a plaque now hangs above his favorite booth) before going un-gently into the night.

But the woeful stories, like the gladdening ones, are absorbed in the social history, and ripen it. If today the Village is not the place it once was—the single glittering capital of American bohemia—it remains the cultural enclave most richly nourished by the past. This is the meaning of social history, as Henry James understood. It is why, as an old man, made uneasy by a new century, estranged from a homeland no longer truly his, he savored in all their dishevelment the unchanged streets of his childhood. They had lasted and that was enough.

And it is why four decades later, Alfred Kazin, an immigrant son of Brooklyn in the first flush of literary success, could feel at home in "the crooked streets leading past so many little nineteenth-century houses." No ancestors of Kazin had lived in those venerable quarters, and yet

> I always had a sense of coming into my own, of enjoying some special intimacy with lower Fifth Avenue that made me think of Henry Adams's *Esther* posing for the mural in the Church of the Ascension on Fifth and Tenth, of Mark Twain in his old house on Tenth Street, Dreiser and Millay in Washington Square, Willa Cather on Bank Street.

Like all true forebears, these giants endure as living presences, abiding spirits, and anyone who really means to can find them. They still inhabit the cramped flats, still quarrel in the dark bistros, still haunt the fabled streets that wind as trickily as memory itself. They endure, in sum, in the built environment of Greenwich Village, in its huddled structures and open spaces.

To explore this singular community, birthplace of so much that has enriched our culture, is to travel multiple routes that lead, step by step, into the recesses of the past. It is a past that forms the foundation, for better or worse, of the future we create.

◆

Old Greenwich Village

AN ARCHITECTURAL PORTRAIT

The White Horse Tavern, Hudson and 11th Streets, founded 1880.

Marie's Crisis Café, 59 Grove Street, takes its name from "The Crisis," a pamphlet by revolutionist Tom Paine, who died here in 1809.

Cornelia Street Café, 29 Cornelia Street.

Old Homestead, 56 Ninth Avenue, established 1868.

Bigelow Pharmacy building, 414 Sixth Avenue, built 1902.

The Strand, Broadway and 12th Street—"eight miles of books."

Pathfinder Mural (1989), Charles and West Streets—the collective work of eighty artists from twenty countries.

Flea market at playground of Public School 41, Greenwich Avenue and Charles Street.

Sculptures in Christopher Park (at Sheridan Square) commemorate the beginning of Gay activism in 1969, when Villagers protested a police raid on the Stonewall Inn, a tavern on the square.

Union Square at 14th Street—long the rallying ground of agitators, now home to vendors.

Washington Square
Park viewed from
6 Washington
Square North.

Corner Bistro, West 4th and Jane Streets.

Washington Arch at Washington Square. Erected in 1892, this limestone-faced structure replicates and replaces a wooden one designed 16 years earlier by McKim, Mead & White.

70 Barrow Street.

396 Bleecker Street.

Houses on St. Luke's Place date from the early 1850s. In the 1920s, Mayor James J. Walker lived at Number 6; novelists Sherwood Anderson and Theodore Dreiser at 12 and 16, respectively.

Arbor and birdhouse, 121 Charles Street.

Mid-19th-century houses on Grove Street.

319 West 13th Street.

1850s houses on Bleecker Street.

347 West 12th Street.

View of Bleecker Street from Seventh Avenue South.

Original PureOil gas station
on Seventh Avenue South
(near Commerce Street),
built 1927.

45

Village Community Church (1846), 143 West
13th Street—now converted to residences.

11 Commerce Street.

18 Commerce Street.

30 Grove Street.

"The Row," 1830s Greek Revival buildings on Washington Square North, once housed many distinguished New Yorkers: the Delano family, Edith Wharton, Edward Hopper.

Grove Court—known as "Mixed Ale Alley" when laborers at local breweries lived here in the 1850s.

Garden at 19 Barrow Street.

Patchin Place, off West 10th Street near Sixth Avenue—home at various times to John Reed, e.e. cummings, Djuna Barnes.

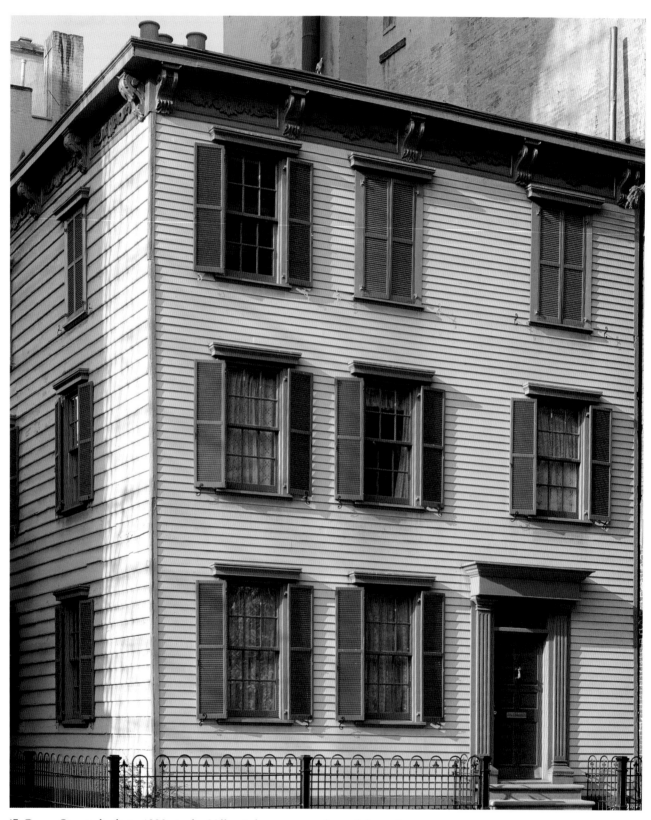

17 Grove Street, built in 1822, is the Village's best-preserved wood-frame house.

7 Leroy Street—an archetypal Federal rowhouse.

17 Grove Street (see page 52).

The Hair Place, 77 Perry Street.

28 and 30 West 10th Street, part of the "English Terrace Row" (1856-58) attributed to architect James Renwick, Jr. Artist Marcel Duchamp lived at Number 28; novelist Sinclair Lewis at 37.

16-18 Charles Street.

114 Waverly Place.

Corner of Waverly Place and Bank Street.

Ty's Bar, 114 Christopher Street.

The Cherry Lane Theatre, 38 Commerce Street, founded in 1924 by Edna St. Vincent Millay and friends.

Le Figaro Café, 186 Bleecker Street.

Washington Mews, between University Place and Fifth Avenue. These residences once served as stables for houses on Washington Square.

The Cowgirl Hall of Fame, 519 Hudson Street.

Chumley's, 86 Bedford Street. Speakeasy of choice among Village literati from Theodore Dreiser to John Dos Passos to Saul Bellow. Its name is still not posted.

The Lion's Head Inn, 59 Christopher Street.

The Cooper Union, Astor Place and East 8th Street, founded in 1859. A prominent school of art and architecture and the nation's oldest steel-beam building.

Inauguration Day 1993 at the Dew Drop Inn, Greenwich Avenue and Perry Street.

Caffe Reggio, 119 MacDougal Street—the Village's first coffeehouse, opened in 1927.

El Faro Restaurant, 823 Greenwich Street.

Minetta Tavern, 113 MacDougal Street.

Inside the White Horse Tavern (see page 23). A plaque is mounted above Dylan Thomas's booth.

Universal Grill, 44 Bedford Street.

Tea and Sympathy, 108 Greenwich Avenue.

Caffe Maurizio, 434 Hudson Street.

Casa Di Pre Restaurant, corner of West 4th and West 12th Streets.

McManus Florist, 69 Eighth Avenue.

Produce and flower market, Sullivan and West 3rd Streets.

498 LaGuardia Place near Houston Street.

Garber's Hardware, 49 Eighth Avenue, founded 1884.

Willie Cascio's shoe repair, 320 Bleecker Street.

U.S.E.D. Antiques, 17 Perry Street.

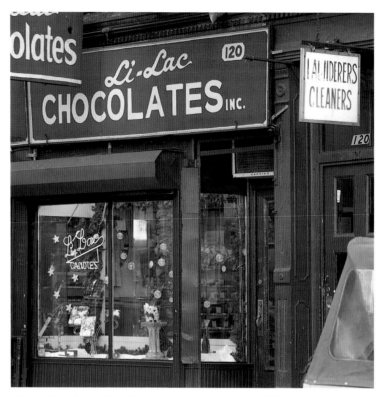

Li-Lac Candies, 120 Christopher Street—since 1923.

Taylor's Pastry, 523 Hudson Street.

A Different Light Bookstore, 548 Hudson Street.

The three-sided Northern Dispensary, 165 Waverly Place, built in 1831. Closed in 1989, this free clinic served indigent Villagers since its founding in 1827. Edgar Allan Poe was once treated here.

Conservative Synagogue of Fifth Avenue, 11 East 11th Street.

14 West 10th Street—home to Mark Twain and his family in the early 1900s.

George Washington on Washington Arch (1892) by sculptor Alexander Stirling
Calder, father of mobile-maker Alexander "Sandy" Calder.

Courtyard of Grace Church (1846), Broadway and 10th Street—a jewel of neo-Gothic design by
James Renwick, Jr.

Cemetery of Congregation Shearith Israel, founded 1805, West 11th Street just east of 6th Avenue.

41 Commerce Street.

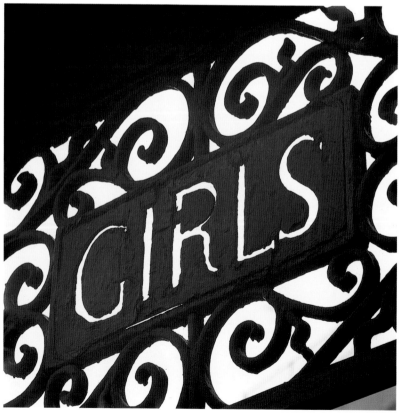

Village Community School, 272 West 10th Street.

Number 6 Washington Square North.

Federal Archives Building, 641 Washington Street, from the garden of St. Luke-in-the-Fields Church. This massive Romanesque-style structure dates from 1899.

Christopher Park at Sheridan Square, which is named after Civil War General Philip Henry Sheridan.

View east from rooftop of the New School for Social Research, 66 West 12th Street.

Jackson Square Park, Greenwich Avenue and Horatio Street.

The Family (1979) by Chaim Gross, West 11th and Bleecker Streets.

Portrait of Sylvette by Pablo Picasso (executed by Carl Nesjar) within University Village (1966), an apartment complex designed by I.M. Pei.

The Sheridan Square Viewing Garden at the intersection of Washington Place, West Fourth, and Barrow Streets.

Fire Patrol Number 2, 84 West Third Street, built 1906.

Novasac Building, 416 West 13th Street.

107 Waverly Place.

Colonnade Row, 428-434 Lafayette Street, completed in 1833. Astors, Delanos, and Vanderbilts occupied residences secluded by these Corinthian columns.

Above and opposite: The Joseph Papp Public Theater, originally the Astor Library (1853-81), was founded in 1967 by Papp as the New York Shakespeare Festival. The building now accommodates six performance spaces.

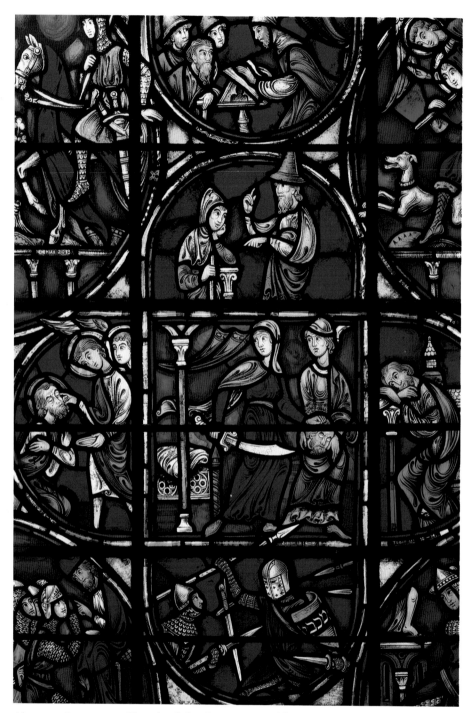

Above and opposite: Church of the Ascension, Fifth Avenue and 10th Street, synthesizes the work of some of America's best 19th-century architects, artists, and craftsmen: Richard Upjohn (architecture), John LaFarge (altar mural), LaFarge and Louis Comfort Tiffany (stained-glass windows), Augustus Saint-Gaudens (altar relief), and McKim, Mead & White (interior remodeling).

Church of St. Luke in the Fields, a true country church, built in 1822 when Greenwich was a rural hamlet. Opposite: The interior was renovated following a fire in 1981.

The Salmagundi Club, founded in 1870, is the nation's oldest artists' club and has occupied the former Irad Hawley residence (1853) at 47 Fifth Avenue since 1917. The library (opposite) is trimmed with palettes and mugs of members. Former club president Kenneth Fitch sits among portraits of other past presidents.

First Presbyterian Church (1846), Fifth Avenue at 11th Street, designed by Joseph C. Wells.

43 Fifth Avenue.

This page and opposite: The Old Merchant's House, 29 East 4th Street, built in 1832—an authentic remnant of the Federalist era.

Above and opposite: Residence of designer Michael Russo, MacDougal Alley.

Artist Barton Benes in his studio, Westbeth Artists' Housing, 155 Bank Street.

Clay studio at the New York Studio School of Drawing, Painting and Sculpture, 8 West 8th Street. Formerly the site of the Whitney Museum of American Art, John Sloan and Reginald Marsh held their first solo exhibitions here.

Hearth (1918) by artist Robert Winthrop Chanler in Gertrude Vanderbilt Whitney's studio, 17½ MacDougal Alley, now part of the New York Studio School (see preceding page).

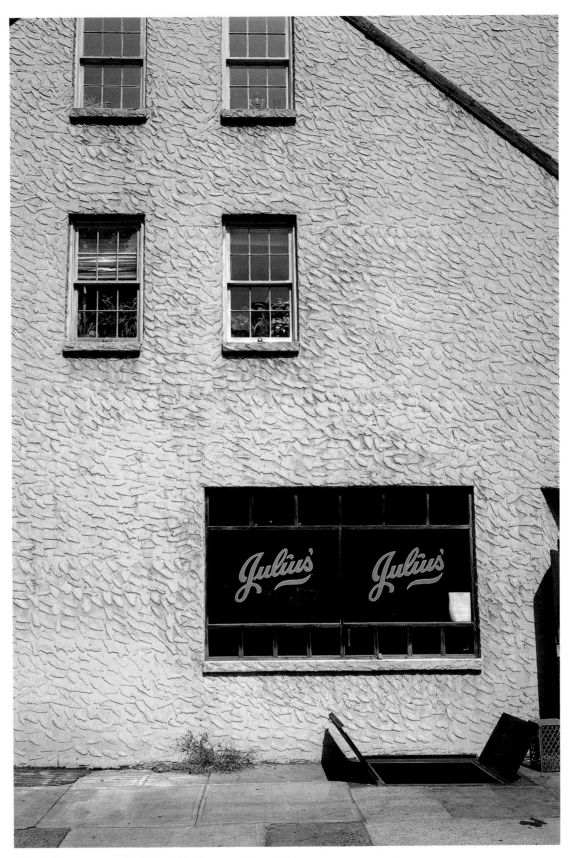

Julius' Restaurant, 159 West 10th Street—since 1864.

Classroom at the New School for Social Research (1930), 66 West 12th Street, designed by Joseph Urban. Murals are by José Clemente Orozco.

Marshall Chess Club, 23 West 10th Street, established 1915.

Jefferson Market Courthouse (1877), Sixth Avenue and 10th Street. This exuberant Victorian assemblage by Vaux & Withers now houses a branch of the New York Public Library.

LaGuardia Corner Gardens on LaGuardia Place.

Above and opposite: Clocktower of the Jefferson Market Courthouse (see page 116).

Pier 52 off Gansevoort Street—the Hudson River defines the Village's western boundary.

Vendor's stall at Gansevoort Meat Market, Washington and 13th Streets.

11th Street and University Place.

One Fifth Avenue, built 1929.

Door to hall and tower of Judson Memorial Baptist Church (1892), 53 Washington Square South, by McKim, Mead & White.

The John L. Tishman Auditorium of the New School for Social Research (1930), 66 West 12th Street, designed by Joseph Urban.

Selected Bibliography

William Barrett. *The Truants: Adventures Among the Intellectuals.* Garden City, New York: Anchor/Doubleday, 1982.

Saul Bellow. *Humboldt's Gift.* New York: Viking, 1975.

Malcolm Cowley. *A Second Flowering: Works and Days of the Lost Generation.* New York: Viking, 1973.

——— ———. *Exile's Return: A Literary Odyssey of the 1920s.* New York: Viking, 1979.

Edmund T. Delaney and Charles Lockwood. *Greenwich Village: A Photographic Portrait.* New York: Dover, 1976.

Andrew S. Dolkart. *Guide to New York City Landmarks.* Washington, DC: National Trust, 1992.

John Dos Passos. *1919.* New York: Harcourt, Brace, 1961.

Theodore Draper. *The Roots of American Communism.* New York: Viking, 1957.

Susan Edmiston and Linda D. Cirino. *Literary New York: A History and Guide.* Boston: Houghton Mifflin, 1976.

Paul Goldberger. *The City Observed: New York.* New York: Vintage, 1979.

Harmon H. Goldstone and Martha Dalrymple. *History Preserved: A Guide to New York City Landmarks and Other Districts.* New York: Shocken, 1979.

Granville Hicks. *John Reed: The Making of a Revolutionary.* New York: Macmillan, 1936.

Henry James. *Washington Square.* New York: Dell, 1959.

——— ———. *The American Scene.* Bloomington, Indiana: Indiana University, 1968.

Alfred Kazin. *New York Jew.* New York: Vintage, 1979.

Terry Miller. *Greenwich Village and How It Got that Way.* New York: Crown, 1990.

Museum of the City of New York. "Within Bohemia's Borders: Greenwich Village, 1830 to 1930." New York, 1990.

Lincoln Steffens. *The Autobiography of Lincoln Steffens.* New York: Harcourt, Brace, 1931.

Lionel Trilling. *A Gathering of Fugitives.* Boston: Beacon, 1956.

Steven Watson. *Strange Bedfellows: The First American Avant-Garde.* New York: Abbeville, 1991.

Norval White and Elliot Willensky. *AIA Guide to New York City.* New York: Macmillan, 1978.

Walt Whitman. *The Complete Poems.* New York: Penguin, 1971.

Edmund Wilson. *The Shores of Light.* Boston: Northeastern University, 1985.

Paul Zweig. *Walt Whitman.* New York: Basic, 1984.

Index

Acknowledgments

For their generous support:

Barton Benes

Avis Berman

Kathy Bonomi

Mel Byars

L. Cohen

Laury Egan

Kenneth Fitch

Lorinda Fraser

Jack & Ernie Gross

Hilda Holyer

Buckley Jeppson

Regina Kellerman

Tuli Kupferberg

Mindy Lang

Miriam Lee

Scott Marshall

James Owen Mathews

Carolyn Maxwell

Mitzi & Bernie Mayer

Douglas Morgan

Elise Quasebarth

Michael Russo

Edith Saldinger

Deborah Styles

Lydia Tanenhaus

Gladys & Morrison Tucker

Iren Tucker

Janet Walker

Lauren Wisbauer

Martin Wong

John Wynne